Praise

I have a complicated relationship with poetry but not with Darlene Young's poetry. Her poetry laser beams into my mind and winds around my soul.

The poems in *Here* are no exception. They are steeped in lived experience—pure, raw, emotion well-wrought. I see them and feel them and even when I don't completely relate to them I understand them. Yes, their themes and images, but also the form of them: why they exist in the way they do. And this is just as true of the humorous poems as the poignant poems, and the angry poems, and the wistful poems. Above all, *Here* solidifies Young's status as Mormon Literature's great chronicler of the mortal body: of adolescence and aging; of the feminine and the masculine; of power and weakness; of fear, sickness, and simple pleasure; of the inevitable march of time; of what it is to live in this here (and this now).

—William Morris

author of *The Darkest Abyss: Strange Mormon Stories*

and *Dark Watch and other Mormon-American Stories*

Darlene Young's voice is full of wit, self-deprecation, and a wide range of emotions punctuated with enthusiasm as she talks to God as a child and to her sons as a mother. Is she "driving the day, or being driven?" Both, it seems, because "each morning God . . . extends his hand." She takes it, and lets it guide her through motherhood and middle-age knowing that he is with her, even "in the ache."

— Marilyn Bushman-Carlton

author of *on keeping things small* and *Her Side of It*

Darlene Young keeps a record of the things that matter. Nothing is inconsequential to her poetic eye. Friends, neighbors, sons, and husbands take part on this plane where the sacred and the simple meet. God is here, too, moving in and out of Young's poetic lines like the wind in John 3:8, which blows wherever it pleases. A teenager shovels snow and get his driver's license, a mom treasures holy moments of the ordinary, a husband and wife age together through friction and faith. Through it all, Young testifies of a God who listens and heals, but—in his wisdom—not always. In the world created by her poetic vision, we see that the Good News is everywhere, even if we only catch it in glimpses.

—Jack Harrell
author of *Caldera Ridge* and
A Sense of Order and Other Stories

Darlene Young's *Here* is a hymn to "this jumblesale world," a journey into middle-aged motherhood, into empty nesting, into God. While a youngest son is on the cusp of manhood, and a mother who worries if she's done enough to prepare him for life, God shows up each morning as dance partner and "jerks / his head meaningfully towards the dance floor." Her response: a "hell yes." The voice in these poems is often playful and laced with refreshing snark, such as when she says no to addressing God as "Thou" instead of "You" in her prayers. Other times the speaker's voice is earnest-honest, such as when she considers her heartbreak over her son's heartbreak: "Either way, / it's you with your hand outstretched, / longing." *Here* is hyper-aware of the moment, ultra-attentive to the now—at the cusp of letting grown children go, noting the body's slow fumble into age—we're reminded that all we have is fleeting, temporary, and therefore incredibly precious. We are gently transformed.

—Dayna Patterson
author of *O Lady, Speak Again*

Praise for Darlene Young

…she has provided exemplary art that makes use of both the loftiness of our eternal doctrines and our humble and fumbling daily efforts to live up to them.

—Citation for the 2022 Association for Mormon Letters
Smith-Pettit Foundation Award for
Outstanding Contribution to Mormon Letters

Young, during a golden era of Mormon poets publishing provocative work, writes of everyday life as a "Utah Mormon" with language that elevates the mundane to the heroic and the beautiful. *Homespun and Angel Feathers* quietly sits among its peers with less flash or surface difficulty, yet it more directly, consistently, and deeply engages with themes and paradoxes of Latter-day Saint life—all while maintaining a surface friendly to casual readers who simply want a spot of pleasure from beautiful language, easily understood.

— Citation for the 2019 Association for Mormon Letters
Potery Prize for *Homespun and Angel Feathers*

here

BCC PRESS

BY COMMON CONSENT PRESS is a non-profit publisher dedicated to producing affordable, high-quality books that help define and shape the Latter-day Saint experience. BCC Press publishes books that address all aspects of Mormon life. Our mission includes finding manuscripts that will contribute to the lives of thoughtful Latter-day Saints, mentoring authors and nurturing projects to completion, and distributing important books to the Mormon audience at the lowest possible cost.

here

Darlene Young

For information contact
By Common Consent Press
4900 Penrose Dr.
Newburgh, IN 47630

Cover design: D Christian Harrison
Photo credit: Angela Bailey via Unsplash
Book design: Andrew Heiss

www.bccpress.org

ISBN-13: 978-1-948218-88-7

10 9 8 7 6 5 4 3 2 1

For Roger,
who made me forever Young,
and who bought me that first laptop

Contents

I   . . . jostle and jounce . . .   1

Investigative Journalism   3
Over the Top   4
Lone and Dreary: First Argument   5
Forgive Me   6
My Son in the Kitchen After School   7
Shoveling I: 4th Ward Priests Quorum Assignment   8
My Teenager's Braces: Variations   10
Why I Chose to Become a Parent   13
My Son Sings in the High School Choir and Sounds Good   15
Learner's Permit   16
The Young Men Go River Rafting for a Week   18
I Explain Middle Age to my Forebears Who Died Young   19
Morning Jog, Age 49   21

II   . . . winter lurking in the wings . . .   23

Lone and Dreary: First Dis-ease   25
Dear Groundhog, February 2021   26
2020 Politics at the Family Gathering: A Mirror Poem   27
Lone and Dreary: After the First Burnt Offering   28
A Plan of Salvation   29
The Truth Is   30

My Friend's Marriage is Failing, But I'm Not Supposed to Know 33

Her Biopsy 34

The Afternoon Wanes 35

A Good Sick Girl Never Gives Up 37

What I Have Learned 39

Ground 42

Christmas 43

After the Fire, Be Still My Soul 45

III . . . this jumblesale world . . . 47

Kite 49

Shoveling II: 5 a.m., Salt Lake City Suburb 50

It's Time for My Son to Decide Whether to Serve a Mission 52

Abraham Lets Lot Choose His Inheritance 54

Two Weeks After Your Mission Call, You Get Angry 55

Lone and Dreary: Cain Comes Home from the Field 56

Replacing the Carpet in the Emptying Nest 58

What Her Missionary Son's Letter Didn't Say 60

Flood 61

Tower of Babel 63

We Go Camping During a Pandemic 64

To My College Kids, Back at Home Because of Covid 65

Launch 67

Hot Flash 68

IV   . . . its glorious burn . . .   69

Jane, While Beth   71
At Age 50, She Buys Pink Roller-Skates   72
Mother's Day in the Spirit World   74
Your Broken Heart Over Your Son's Broken Heart   75
A Prayer   76
Prayer Language   77
Temples in the Temple   78
Watching My Husband Play Softball   80
Date Night is Takeout and Netflix   81
Heading to the Cabin, Heber, Utah   83
The Refrigerator Clicks On   84
God as a Verb   86
The Mirrored Ball Never Gets Taken Down   87

Notes   89
Acknowledgements   91

Here I am in the garden laughing
an old woman with heavy breasts
and a nicely mapped face

—Grace Paley, "Here"

|

. . . jostle and jounce . . .

Investigative Journalism

I n the sunrise this morning, and in the hallelujahs of the dang
   magpies
W aking me to it. In the oatmeal, so earnest and filling.
I n the warmth of my beloved's hand as we pray over it, and in the
L uminous, messy-haired teenager who sleeps on his arms at the
   table with us.
L ord, I will find you out. And I will report. I will
T ake notes as you speak. The geese against the sky. The easy
R umble of the car starting when I forgot to warm it up early, but
A lso, on the day it doesn't, your hum that abides, though I
N iggle and fret in search of the frequency. In the way a friend
S tays when I tell her the hard thing. And, when she doesn't, in the
C lear-cut path my injury harrows between you and me. I will
R eceive. Some days you speak and my pain eases. Some days
I t doesn't, but you abide in the ache. You radiate. I am
B athed in your transmissions, all of them pure, though my fear
E ncrypts them. I will battle the static. I'll resist the what-if and
   the not-
Y et, the two-week delay for results of the biopsy.
O, let me calibrate. I will tweak and tune and modulate,
U nencumber myself from slurry and slouch. And then I will write.

Here.

Over the Top

At first light it was the birds against the sky
in the frame of the window I'd left uncovered like open hands,
like a bucket set out to catch rain,
and you delivered, Lord,
like a casserole brought to the door
by lipsticked church ladies. All this
to get me out of bed—

you're pulling out all the stops! Then,
practically giftwrapped,
a cat, braiding purrs around my ankles,
got me down the stairs. You're not playing fair.

Now, as the day and I face off, I wonder:
am I driving the day or being driven?
You lure me, Lord. Almost devilishly,
you drop breadcrumbs,
and I follow, bewitched.

Lone and Dreary: First Argument

An ache like a seed
caught in teeth, acrid after-
taste of unripe fruit;

astonishment. *That
is not what I meant.* Sudden
drop of a gaze, new

heaviness. *Where are
you going?* Strange entrapment
within skin, like the tree-

gum that had to be
cut from Eve's hair. *I
just didn't hear you.*

The twitch of a brow.
She remembers the bitterness
of a beetle crunched

accidentally, hidden in the spinach;
she remembers
the first rasp of ivy rash on the wrist.

*Look at me
when I'm talking.* Heart pounding
in her ears. A shoulder

shrugs away from a hand. Skin
is not just for pleasure; it
can chafe. She is learning

what a weed is,
and what it does.

Forgive Me

It's just that it was that kind of day,
the kind of day in which the cat moved from room to room,
the kind of day in which the sink drain gave off strange smells,
the kind of day in which the space between people was heavy as
     water, and pale, by which I mean the space between you and me.
It was an itchy kind of day. The bruise of routine.
It was the kind of day in which trees bent toward each other to
     whisper bad news and the earth turned its shoulder against us
     and all we stood for.
It was the kind of day in which dirty snow couldn't hide, though
     it looked away,
the kind of day in which birds sat lonely in bare trees, or agitated
     together in gnarled clumps.
I wanted to unzip my flesh, step out and walk around, dissolve
     into the sky.
It was the kind of day in which my hands rifled through each
     other, searching,
the kind of day in which traffic clotted and oozed fretfully, by
     which I mean the traffic between you and me.
It was the kind of day in which the air carried laughter from the
     distant school, metallic laughter, raw—
laughter from other people's children.
What we bump against, overlook, underplay, creates layer upon
     layer of shellac.
It was a mop kind of day. The wind and the clock and the drip
     and the mail and the gutter.
It was the kind of day in which I kept catching you at the edge of my
     vision, by which I mean that you were almost there but not there.
It was the kind of day in which what I meant wasn't what I said nor
     what I meant to say, which is to say that it was just that kind of day.

My Son in the Kitchen After School

I say it looks like he could use a haircut
      and he ducks, touching his head, looking away.

The girls like it this way, he says, on his way out,
      and I'm wondering what girls, picturing

those little bimbos with too much makeup, but
      they are good girls, I know.

Looks like I've done it again. I meant to say
      he is miraculous. He

has a whole universe I will never know about,
      and it is big and it is important and I want

to tell him that I know this but I'm whispering now
      to myself in the quivering space he's left

behind. "Listen," I say to myself, "just because
      you can still see him doesn't mean your road

and his aren't angling apart and no amount of lying
      in the dirt can pull them back together into

one path and you and I both know you wouldn't have it so."
      "Yes," I say, "but would it be so bad to have our paths

be parallel, just a little longer, just until—oh I don't know—"
      but my voice is tinny and I've stopped listening.

Shoveling I: 4th Ward Priests Quorum Assignment

A tall and sleep-heavy boy with hair in his eyes
has left his lonely trail of footprints in the dark
of 5 a.m. to the driveway he's been assigned
to relieve of snow.
                        Underdressed
for the cold as required of his age and gender
he clutches his shovel in despair at the discovery
that his work partner has slept in, leaving him alone
with his god.
                        Dreamlike,
the heft of spade becomes a yoga, endless pant
and dig, sisyphean. He can't remember
anything else—the jolt of the summertime track
beneath sneakers, the school cafeteria, even
the Sunday world of suits and hymns.
There has never been another world than this
Martian landscape, no other light than this
metallic star-lit buzz.
                        This mindless rhythm
thins time, which spins in glittering wrinkles around him,
small center of spiraling galaxies, shoveling.

After an eon his head comes up; it's time
to get ready for school and he is not half done.
A dog barks somewhere.

He pictures the old lady who lives here,
her shuffle at church, the way she lowers
herself into the pew. He imagines her opening
her door later today to a half-finished driveway.

He imagines another tardy on his record.
Surely a neighbor will come by with a snowblower.

He shovels a little more as he ponders manhood
and shame.
                              Sometimes
he thinks he glimpses a man, the man he might become.
He drags towards that man like a deep-diver
for the surface; the water pulling him down
is his own body heavy with sleep and lust
and bottomless hunger.

                              The clear, cold air.
He stills himself and hears the beginning of morning
traffic, people going places. Someday,
he will go places, too—

                              or maybe not. Maybe
he will disappear in a puff of COVID-19,
or a North Korean missile, or the brown smog
that covers everything these days and will soon make
even this fresh, young snow

                              murky and rank.
How it weighs on him, how it will smother everything.

But not yet.
This morning is clear and sharp. The work
is what is in front of him. He takes up his shovel again,
greeting the dawn with his breath.

My Teenager's Braces: Variations

1.
You bit me with tooth buds when nursing.
You bit me with milkteeth at four. These days,
we bite at each other. The only thing here I can tame
            is this underbite.

2.
The way teeth can enter rooms before you,
you race to grow up. The human race
demands straight teeth, but here's
a tiny   silver   picket   fence
to keep the girls off for a few more years.
            I don't mind.

3.
My first boyfriend
had darling crooked front teeth.
By straightening yours, do I teach you
to overlook the joy of *whatever*
is fickle, freckled, adazzle, dim?

4.
I brace myself
against your future.

You brace yourself
against your genes,
            against history,
            against any path
            that bores you,

buck at the boundaries,
balk at my embrace.

5.
Growth within bounds. Your parents
        are the gums—soft around the bone and root—
                that you grow out of.

6.
"Avoid sticky foods," they say.
I worry at night about what is stuck
to you,
in you.
Between us.

7.
The orthodontist says
you can use wax to soften the edges.
        Don't.
Let your tender inner tissues
toughen up.

Once the bands are gone,
your teeth will feel slimy.
        Slippery freedom.

8.
You complain you must spend time re-learning
how to play your trumpet. I say
it's worthwhile to learn about something you love
from a different angle.

9.
Your father, the son of a dentist,
would not be your father

had I not spent time in braces myself.
My naturally crooked teeth are not
your parents' only secret from the world.
We are committed.
We leave much unsaid.

10.
Your rare smile last night—
my eyes watered
in the bracing air.

Why I Chose to Become a Parent

Because potato bugs.
Because of the way stars look
when viewed from a lap, a blanket
tucked under chins.

Because small-talk in the post office,
and lit windows at night,
and the shadows that cross them.
Velcro. Cookie dough.

Because of the way, when I was four,
the raindrops chased each other sideways
on the backseat window
on the way home from Grandma's.

The taste of old pennies,
train whistles in the distance.
"The Monster Mash."
Milkweed.

Because of the old man who plays Santa
at the church dinner every year.

Because perpetual motion machines
and playing cards tacked to the spokes of bikes.
Because marshmallows.

Because of little girls in tutus carrying light sabers.
And little boys in tutus, too. And rainboots.
Kites.
Because of the way a mother quail leads me
away from her nest.

Because of the evenings my father played
the ukelele in the living room
and my sisters and I danced,
ribbons streaming from our fingers,
spinning ourselves breathless.

Because, 40 years later, I still remember
the scent of my mother.

My Son Sings in the High School Choir and Sounds Good

Mostly all grown up, the cuffs of your suit pants a little
too short. You lose yourself in the music, eyes intent
on the director but you steal a glance at me, fight
a small smile. You know you sound good, and you
know I know it. You feel the joy of disappearing
into music, creating a column of butterflies that dances
on people's faces like water crystal, the joy of creating
something where there was nothing, the way a mother
creates a boy, the way a man comes into being
where there was a boy before, leaving lonely tracks
behind him. Once, in kindergarten, you threw up,
and your teacher made you stand there in the sick
for twenty minutes, all eyes on you, until I could arrive.
Your eyes on me then triggered a fury in me
towards that teacher bigger than I'd ever felt before,
a lust almost for violence, leaving me bewildered
to know myself truly. You glance at me now
with those same eyes, but that memory just here
feels like a betrayal, and I need to leave the building
to give you some space.

Learner's Permit

No getting out
of this one. Who else can do this
but the person who knows the state of this boy's underwear,
or how he wept for hours that time he saw the injured cat
pull itself to the ditch?
Look how he expects the universe to part for him
like a youtube celebrity on the dancefloor. The cheek of it,
fair, downy cheek!
Is that cologne you smell on him?
Bite your tongue, babe
is your leitmotif from here on out
for this strapping stranger.
Remember LaMaze? Short breaths. Strap
yourself in, mama, slide your seat back, because this ride
ain't over. It will never be over, not even once
he's pulled into the garage
and you ooze yourself out of there,
jaw aching from the clench of it,
gut-braiding bowel-clutch and wrench of it.
This ride's just begun, honey, one long road
stretching to the horizon, Highway of Hotfoot,
Parturition Parkway, Sayonara Street.
You get a year or two of profile and then it's all
back pockets and dust. White-knuckle
it out. Haul him intact through these next few years
like a football tucked under your arm;
that's what's left for you and it'll take

all you've got. Pray to your dead mother,
who surely has forgiven you by now, who
of course accepts your assignment
as angel of teen drivers—yes, pray to her,
in her smug told-you-so, and pray to his future
children, can't you just see them now,
towheaded and dear. So desperately
wide-eyed and dear.

The Young Men Go River Rafting for a Week

*What can I say but stay
alive?*
                    —Maggie Smith

I'm channeling Sariah, she who let
the men (her husband and her God) proclaim
that though that trip back could have been avoided if
they had just thought ahead, it's actually
what had been intended all along.
"Certain struggles can change boys to men."

For *these* boys there are no brass plates
whose worth could change the world,
no future civilization that depends
on the heroic sacrifice of phones
and showers for a week. And so
the men have found some artificial task,

this danger-sold-as-entertainment, twinkies
and adrenaline its trimmings. The leaders
downplay the danger but I'm not fooled.
Sometimes they don't come home. I see
the headlines every year or so—"Scout killed
on outing." I picture Lehi patting Sariah's
hand—"They'll be fine, dear." Sariah's boys

were gone for weeks and in the end
came home triumphant, yes, but scarred,
the dearest one learning to live with blood
on his hands. The test is also for the mom.
I'm left to wrestle through the week:
what do I want, and what can I let go?

I Explain Middle Age to my Forebears Who Died Young

For Jane, age 34, and Sharla, age 43

Dear Mama and Grandma,
I transcribe your losses.

First, behold the Middle Aged Body,
land of the slump. All the flesh,
the neckflesh, the buttocks,
listing toward its future grave.
The trick knee, the missing words. You
who never had to dye your hair,
behold the applicator tube, the bloody rinse.
Behold the hot flash,
the strangle of clammy clothes,
the kicked-away sheets.

So much for the body.
But lo, there are other things.

Older children who call over their shoulders
as they leave, or surprise you
by presenting a cheek for a kiss.
The gentle hands of a long-time lover
and his tender new wrinkles.
The creeping, sore-muscled joy of knowing
you've been taken to the dance, whirled and dined—
the whole shebang.

The opening of hands over the river that is time
to drop what you've clung to,

see it splash and bob away,
gentle denouement. A comfortable
chair in the afternoon, an old coat that lasts.

Let's tally it up. You've missed
nothing, and
the whole world.

Morning Jog, Age 49

Hoist and stagger,
jostle and jounce,
each thrust of thighs a whale-
song call to a buoyancy long past.
My years jangle in the joints.
Old jar of bones, jug
sludging while the sleek
barrel by, glittering, glancing
back with pity. Pitted,
rusty, dull plodding blunt
tool that I am, I push
forward, butting
the earth. From above,
I would appear to ooze
around this track, not ungelatinous.
Slogging around at ground-level
I picture myself inching
across the landscape of my years:
slow progress
in increments of breaths.
Was I ever fleet? My life,
my children—all has blown past.
Whiplashed, gasping, still
I trundle.

II

. . . winter lurking in the wings . . .

Lone and Dreary: First Dis-ease

It comes an hour after
the first gluttony
(sudden riot of blueberries,
such a frantic sucking in,
now that she knew
things could be lost).

The sense
of the world listing, off-
kilter. Clamminess, the blister
of sweat on her face,
between her breasts.
Dead-salmon swollen,
she pants as something
rises, roiling, a-swarm inside.
Claustrophobia of flesh,
gullet-choking, kaleidoscopic
surge, urge to turn
inside-out.
She holds still,
terrorized by jostle.

But chores await.
She sloshes and oozes
as she gathers firewood,
grasping at trees,
not knowing what will pass
and when.
The panic of open-endedness.
She thinks, *This new and terrible world,*
so many ways to stumble
forward in the dark.

Dear Groundhog, February 2021

We've been hiding in tunnels for a year,
survivors of an election season sere
enough to make anyone burrow
deeper. Now,
as daylight comes earlier and an inauguration
tilts us towards the sun, we think of nosing
out into the air

just like you. You were called *badger*
in Germany, *groundhog* in Pennsylvania. Elsewhere,
whistle-pig, whistles being your furry version
of the shocked and offended tweet,
warning of danger.

Bear rat, land beaver, weenusk,
red monk. The Algonquian *wuchak*
became *woodchuck*, showing
how cultural misapprehension leads
to fake news—you chuck no wood,
preferring to shear timothy.
Truth is never as dramatic
as rumor. Bury it
and all other inconsistencies
in yesterday's newscycle.

As for other rumors, after
what we've been through this year,
we blink not at the lack of evidence
that what you'll see this morning
matters. We'll find some data somewhere—
just show up and act confident. Then,

please, dear *red monk*, pray for us with fervor.
We need light and air.

2020 Politics at the Family Gathering: A Mirror Poem

you think I think you
your trajectory defines perspective defines trajectory
read from left to right to left, read
truth isn't what isn't truth
dirty hands make hands dirty
he didn't say didn't he
what he did wasn't did he what
if what you heard I what if
you program your news programs you
my news trumps your news trumps my news
what is wrong they say they wrong is what
liars are those who say who those are liars
party defines candidate defines party
that man trumps that man
people count votes count people
power seeps through cracks through seeps power
I think you think I
compromise means progress means compromise
we might together, might we?

Lone and Dreary: After the First Burnt Offering

*And he gave unto them commandments, that they should
worship the Lord their God, and should offer the firstlings of
their flocks, for an offering unto the Lord.*
        —Moses 5:5

*Unto Adam also and to his wife did the Lord God make coats
of skins, and clothed them.*
        —Genesis 3:21

Then the angel showed them what to do
with the rest of the flesh.
"Eat it," he said.
Her mouth watered at the curious smell, but she wept
as she put the greasy chunk to her lips, remembering
her teeth sinking into other strange fruit, remembering
the living lamb.
Later, she was sluggish, gut
roiling at the new work, heart
pounding harder. She saw
there was a mess to clean up,
bones and skin. The angel
showed them what to do with skin, and then
she recognized the clothing she was wearing,
that peculiar parting
gift she had received on the day of banishment.
Skin on skin,
she stood, covered,
digesting death
into life.

A Plan of Salvation

She was born, healthy and bright to the right
family (no trauma, no drama) in a neighborhood healthy
and bright, probably white (no trauma, no drama). Good

clothes, good looks, good music and books, fell in love,
not too soon, lovely wedding, perfect groom, pleasant
little honeymoon. Children came, healthy and bright,

only as often as the parents could afford. They played
together, adored their mother and each other, grew up
without trauma, married without drama to good people

raised right, a delight to their in-laws. And so it proceeded
at just the right pace, well and right, until all that remained
was retirement in a sunny place not too far from the dear

grandchildren, so sweet and polite, healthy and bright,
a spot of golf, a cruise or two, and then she was through,
dying pleasantly in her sleep. And then

she dragged her milky-weak underformed spirit-limbs
into the presence of her god and demanded
her money back.   "Hell,
no!" King Lucifer replied. "You got everything right,
just what you voted for. Sit. Stay. Fetch. Good girl."

The Truth Is

"She never complained."
—innumerable church talks, especially on Mother's Day

1.
She *did* complain, but
her sweet children have chosen
not to remember.
They think this a kindness.

What does such an edit do
to their own wives and daughters,
to themselves?

2.
She *did* complain, but
they didn't notice.
What they heard:
some kind of disturbance
in the distance. It made
them vaguely uneasy,
like when the sun
goes behind a cloud.

3.
She *did* complain, but
well, how does one define *complain*?
They heard wishful thinking,
daydreams—
nothing real.

4.
She did *not* complain.
She didn't know she could.

5.
She did *not* complain.
It was a choice. Unbearable
the thought of herself as complainer.
She'd heard the talks at church.

6.
She did *not* complain.
She had discovered
its fruitlessness.

7.
She did *not* complain.
Those around her would not
allow it. How powerful
their control! How beautiful
their world!

8.
She did *not* complain.
She had lost language completely
in her terror: was this to be
her life?

9.
She did *not* complain,
but kept it inside,
where it ate a hole

through parts of her designed
to protect her from herself.
She went from doctor to doctor
searching.

10.
She did *not* complain.
She had nothing to complain about.
Every day was joyful,
the only problems ones
to which she had the answers,
or bottomless faith that she would soon.
In fact, she's never
left the garden at all.
The adults around her find her amusing.

11.
She did *not* complain,
being silent
like all mythical creatures.

My Friend's Marriage is Failing, But I'm Not Supposed to Know

Two women doing lunch.
A partial list of things
I'm supposed to know about being a woman:
how to wear a scarf, how
to enjoy salad, how to walk in heels,
how to reach across this table
and touch her hand.

Someone across the room
would think we are close—
are we close? She hunches
under her burden but bounces
her voice brightly, all bubbles,
and polka-dots. Nausea
makes my fork heavy. Stupid salad.

I read an article yesterday claiming
people in conversation modulate the music
of their voices: major and minor keys according to the topic, according to their love.

Love is my bringing her here—
though I knew it was simply a front-
row ticket to a performance—and love
is her coming. Which of us is
doing a favor? When I drop her off, watching

her back as she unlocks
her lonely front door, I glance
into my rearview mirror, see
spinach stuck between my two front teeth,
which she must have noticed
and didn't mention.

Her Biopsy

Face-down on a high table, breast wedged
like a ham in the slicer at the deli, she
imagines herself a plastic bag
caught in a sewer grate; a book
dropped carelessly from a hammock, splayed
to the rain—maudlin scenes
soupy with self-pity.
For shame.

Why shame
should think itself invited to this party
she questions only later, after
they've helped her down, said
they'll call with results, shown
her to the lockers. There
she breathes, clutching her blouse,
the fabric nauseating
in its femininity.

The Afternoon Wanes

Autumn powers up like the Las Vegas strip.
You've pulled over onto a golden country road,
beckoned, baited by the hand-painted sign,
"Feed the Fish!" You fall
to the lure, easy detour
from what awaits you, what always awaits you.

Here you are invited to insert a quarter into a machine,
and receive the chance to be a hero. What a bargain!

Tall trees sway as if under the sea, as if waving to God, and God
blows through them and lifts your hair from the neck
of your new orange sweater

that might make you part of the light, melt you
into this place that dazzles
even as the leaves blush in the knowledge of their deaths,
tiny leaf deaths that crunch under your feet,

such happy-sounding deaths.

The sun splashing off the water makes you squint,
a squint being half of a smile, and the decay
around you smells so fresh and happy.
You throw the fish food into the pond

and the pond sizzles, percolates with the pursed lips
of the small spirits that live wet lives, turning
and turning. How jolly! How bright! Children

clap and point to the puckering fish kissing
the surface of the world. Carpe diem, carp!
Such a dancing, bubbling pond,

such a quaint, cute lunge for survival.
You wonder at their joy. You wonder
if they are mostly, usually, starving,

and whether the manna that comes to them from heaven
on shiny fall days when the weather is fortunate
is just enough to preserve their frightful fishy hope

for one more gasping hour at a time.
You get into your car and go home
to the mouths that await you,
winter lurking in the wings.

A Good Sick Girl Never Gives Up

A good sick girl would never give up.
She pushes on in search of a cure,
working as if all depended on her.
"Not knowing beforehand" what she should do,
she moves from doctor to doctor
and test to test, would never rest

    except, of course when money is tight
    (which it always is). A good sick girl
    knows when to stop wasting her family's money
    on that which bears no fruit, the useless pursuit
    of miracle cures

        except, of course, for miracles
        that come from God. She seeks those,
        remembering Sarah who laughed at the angel.
        She adds her name to prayer rolls, requests
        heavy-handed administrations—many,

            except, of course, when it's God's will
            that she not be healed. Then she yields
            her will to God patiently, knowing he
            strengthens the back. She doesn't lack
            that faith. She would never complain

except, of course, to us, her true friends,
her safe space, and we answer with grace
when she asks for help, never notice,
as we drop off our casseroles,
her manicure, the finished novel, though laundry
stacks up and the children run wild.

A good sick girl dresses nicely
for her doctor (would never wallow,
sincerely wants to get well),
but not so neat that he won't believe her
when she says she can't cope.

> Being good, she won't question
> the advice that he gives her,
> obeys his directions in all detail

>> except when he's mistaken, which
>> he often is. And so a good sick girl
>> takes responsibility, researches,
>> follows the Spirit and common sense,

>>> though she would never Google her symptoms
>>> like a hypochondriac, for that proves
>>> negative thinking, something she avoids
>>> like the plague (which she probably
>>> doesn't have—she's checked).

Never would she chase after quacks
and shamans of alternate therapies,
knowing it is a waste of her family's money,
showing a pitiful lack of faith—

> unless it's something God has led her to
> like that guy who helped Aunt Fern—
now *he's* obviously got a God-given gift,
and if the sick girl refuses to give him a chance,
she's being close-minded, just giving up,

>> and a good sick girl never gives up.

What I Have Learned

I. From Water:

Wait. Either

you'll be lifted up

into the air, or

you will settle.

Given time, you'll find

the cracks, the way

beneath

and through,   and out.

Time   wears away what should

be worn away.

When moving, sing,

or laugh, or cry—

your voice

teaches others,

if they care to listen.

Often,

what is unseen, unacknowledged

moves the world.

II. From Stone:

> Even solid things
> sometimes crack. Allowing
> yourself to be used is not shameful
> —if it's your choice. What you are
> is enough. Be it. Sit. You have just
> the right   amount of weight
> in the world. To not claim it
> is to laugh in God's face.

III. From birds:

Don't worry
that winter might
come. It comes. In winter,
take a break. Come back
when you've caught your breath.
Today's song is today's song;
yesterday has nothing to do with it. Trust
that the fledglings are watching:
they'll get what they need.
A tree doesn't run out of room.
End work when you've got
what you need for the day. Sing,
even though it doesn't augment
your income. Sing before work.
Begin the song before the dark
is gone: light is coming; light
is always coming.

Ground

A brown word, like beef made cheap
and easier to cook. As a verb it's a loss
of a chance for flight—a teenager
at the hands of a brown-thinking adult,
or a plane to somewhere else, anywhere else,
the bright and beautiful not-here—
loss for the sake of safety
and all that is reasonable and dull.
It is what you might bounce off of into wild air,
kick against as you swing towards a bluer sky.
A dump for excess electricity.

With *-work* it is the anchor for dreams
that might actually happen. You can
harrow it and seed it, source
of nourishment, like a forthright mother,
wise and sturdy. Some
think it is the not-heaven, a place
we reach from toward God,
but I'm thinking He's here
in the hard-baked cracks of it;

all the best of Him is found
at its level, so to speak.
And when you know Him,
it is what you hit,
running.

Christmas

Once—
in a dirty city on a day
when traffic was especially bad,
a day some people discovered they were out
of flour or clean underwear, and others scraped carrots,
a day someone got married and someone else
broke up loudly, slamming doors, or quietly slipped out
the back; a day someone won a prize, someone walked a colicky
  baby,
two friends offended each other with political comments,
a teenager rolled her eyes; a day which waned like all days
through that itchy hour when you realize you won't finish
what you were supposed to finish today and so
calm yourself with something to drink, maybe,
get through dinner, catch the breeze on a porch
while flies squabble their pettiness—

in a back room, quietly,
something happened.
Here,

while I'm stuck in the snow, the traffic jam,
the aging body, I seek that back room. Here's a clogged
toilet to deal with, a trick knee. I've got to call on that bill
and clean up the groceries I left souring in the trunk, get the
  mammogram,
apologize. My pants don't fit right. The car stalls. But a baby falls
asleep on my shoulder. Someone forgives. A violin calls to me

from a place I almost remember. All these things tell me
of a world that turns toward spring, of things
that happen just out of sight, things that,
quietly, change
everything.

After the Fire, Be Still My Soul

*Now, after the Lord had withdrawn from speaking to me, and
withdrawn his face from me, I said in my heart: Thy servant
has sought thee earnestly; now I have found thee*
            —Abraham 2:12

1.
Between the shockflash of lightning
and the seep-return of sight as the glare fades,
is an electric gasp, an unbodied glimpse
of an existence outside this seasoup of time—
what it must feel like to be God.
And so a child twirls, chin-up to the sky,
then drops to earth, just
to disorient herself.
An attempt at flight,
a reel among the clouds.

2.
As a child trapped
in a body
on a pew
for endless church meetings
I amused myself with a game.
How to play:
open the hymnbook randomly.
Memorize the page number.
With a finger in the book, close it.
Begin a conversation:
What was the page number?
Are you sure?

Are you really sure?
Couldn't it have been 47 instead? 212?
Do not peek.
Do not peek until you are sure that you are sure
no longer.
Do not peek until
you are reeling.

3.
I have put away childish things.
I will resist the thrill of that game,
I will cling to afterimage.
There was lightning. I forbid
the question mark,
though I welcome ellipses.
I will tattoo Thee inside my eyelids,
rehearse Thee and rehearse Thee. I will whisper
Thy name to myself as I fall asleep
so that I wake to Thee. I will keep
forever, my finger in the book.

III

... this jumblesale world ...

Kite

1. Body

Don't resent the tail whipping in the wind; without weight and friction there is no dance. Adjust for sag. Tug and tighten, but know when to ease up. Repair all you can, but remember you can get a new one someday.

2. Marriage

Don't stress over tautness. Tension is what lets you climb. Lean back, trust it, but don't overthink. Look only up and soar.

3. Parenting a Teen

Let out the string. Sometimes even bury the handle for a few minutes while you eat a sandwich. But keep checking the tension. A cavort does not necessarily lead to a crash.

4. God

Does it matter which of you is clutching, which is in sky? Love the tether. Focus on the humming of the string, the tightness of the knots, the glorious bluster of rushing wind. Inhale.

Sing.

Shoveling II: 5 a.m., Salt Lake City Suburb

My son and I walk past the homes of people he's known all his life.
Brother Jackson. The Erdmans. The Schenks. Mrs. Santorini. I make
him recite them. I tell him stories about them. Because he got up
an hour early on this ugly, stale-frost-smelling outer-darkness kind of
  morning,
and I know he's in a precarious position.

He's fifteen. His body aches from overnight growth and he's always
  hungry and he's gained
that sixth sense common to all teenagers: the awareness of hypocrisy.
He knows that there are secrets behind these doors, that all the people
who show up at church each Sunday smiling and clean maybe aren't.
His own roiling chemistry has him suspecting everyone.
I don't think he knows I know this.

He is compliant enough. He gets out of bed because he's been assigned,
and because, in this place, it's what people do. Thank goodness. I've
decided it's a good thing that his body has been trained to obedience.
I know that makes the edge he's walking more sharp—he has more to lose
if he chooses not to believe. But I don't think it's a bad thing

that if he chooses to invest in this religion for the long haul, he already
has the habits. I'm still hoping, though, for the joy. Lo, it percolates,
familiar, in my warming muscles as we begin to shovel old Sister Ames's
driveway. The snow, I see now, glints. It has a presence to it,
like a cat stretched out, waiting. It has its own beauty,

as does Sister Ames, knobbed and gnarled and balding as she is.
Has he glimpsed that yet, this silent son panting near me?
I remember the day I showed up to clean the church building
as a young adult and realized that the place was as much a home to me

as my own house, as familiar. I owned it
as much as anyone.

      The day I realized that many people don't know
what it's like to have a place where so many grown-ups know you,
call you by name, ask after you.

      The day, much later, that I realized that old Sister Bernstein
of the baggy dresses and thick glasses who looked like the middle-aged,
chinless ladies clutching purses in the comics, had been actually *asked*
to lead the music every week, and maybe didn't even want to,
but showed up every week to do it.

Here, I'm grateful to Sister Ames for the thank-you note and candy bar
she sends to my boy for shoveling. I'm grateful for still mornings
when his muscles learn what they are for, though his brain
may take a while to catch up. This is Zion, my boy.
Good morning. Time to wake up.

It's Time for My Son to Decide Whether to Serve a Mission

*"And now it came to pass that all this was done in Mormon,
yea, by the waters of Mormon"*
—Mosiah 18:30

For 18 years I've been forging
this pathway to these waters.
Alma gathered his people,
then asked a question
about commitment,
about going forward.

So here we are. A question
hangs here.
Well?

I've hidden nothing.
You've seen the price
firsthand. And though
you don't realize it yet,
you've also seen the reward.

Yes, what you've seen
is what you get.

So now I ask you—
He asks—we all ask—
is it enough?

Are you full enough now
to spill over?

A beautiful place, this.
In a moment, I might
sit down for a spell.
But first,
let's hear your answer.

Have you? Will you? Can you? Are you?
And did I do enough?
Did I?

Abraham Lets Lot Choose His Inheritance

You're picking out land.
You send out surveyors,
pace the borders. Of course
you seek the inside information, angle
for the head start.

You want it for your kids, right?
The right schools and all that.
As if you could control things.
As if anything were yours,

including the kids.
Listen—

ain't nobody had as tough a start as I,
and even the stars are mine,
though I can't hold them.

Forget logic.
Try to hoard anything
and you lose it.
Burn it for God,
and you'll see it wasn't dear
after all.

In the end, it's about
a voice in the sand—
slippery, sifting—
it's about smoke. A raised hand.

Pitch your tent. Lift
your eyes. By being owned,
own all.

Two Weeks After Your Mission Call, You Get Angry

Your brother pushes you too hard; a wall
gets punched. Ah, that old monster, rage,
whom we've battled together the past
eighteen years. We both know by now
that it will pass. I've learned to wait it out.

But now before me is a vision of you
six months from now, a small apartment
somewhere strange, two young men
imprisoned by the clock and rules
with nowhere else to look but
at themselves.

I share all missionary mothers' fear
of bad companions, having seen the pale
shell-shocked refugees of hate or abuse.
But what if you are the one
who will burden another,
some other mother's boy?
Have I failed you as mother, having failed
to fix your human flaws?

My own flaws, as a human, as a mother,
have broken my heart open to God.
I have tried to teach you this, if nothing else.
And so I send you into the fire. The hope:
that you'll break just barely enough—

break on the dotted line (please, Lord),
leaving you just strength enough
to find the Mender.

Lone and Dreary: Cain Comes Home from the Field

"Were it not for our transgression, we should never have had seed."
—Moses 5:11

Her son comes to her with a different face—
without his brother.
The closest word she's learned
is *winter.*

Without his brother,
blood dripping to his elbows.
Winter:
a time of no fruit.

Blood like her first blood,
that yaw-pang in the womb
as her body prepared to bear fruit,
her own seed.

Now her womb wrenches
at the sight of that blood,
her own seed
looking strange, looking wild.

The shine of slick blood
like juice on his hands
reminds her of the wild, strange
taste of a fruit,

sticky juice on her hand
promising motherhood. So sweet
was the taste of that fruit
she blessed it.

Then, motherhood, sweet
tumble of boys;
she called her choice blessed,
rejoiced at their growth.

The tumble of boys—
and then the horizon.
They grew. Natural, to want
to see for themselves.

Horizon: a mother's fear.
They must be allowed
to see for themselves.
"But be home by dark."

They must be allowed.
"But there are serpents, my sons.
Be home by dark."
Such beautiful boys.

"Serpents, my sons."
A man comes to her with a different face.
Such beautiful boys.
And now she learns *winter.*

Replacing the Carpet in the Emptying Nest

We need less space, but we remodel instead of moving,
holding on to what we can. The family who installed
this ratty shag sold the house in a divorce.
Once, their bare feet explored the spongy glory
now decayed to scratch-and-stiff. Surely by now
we've worn down the bad karma.
New carpet is a parable of hope.

The metal fanged tacks shriek as I yank them
from the shin-barking edges of stairs.
Poofed breaths of dust roil as I tug, dust
made of the flesh of my babies long grown
into lanky boy-men headed out.
How their diapered toddler bottoms bumped
down these stairs; how I carried them
sleeping, back up.

Other things that came down these stairs:
dying pets, three times. Pajama'd children
aglow with Christmas. Me, too many midnights,
checking the driveway for teenagers,
turning off lights.

That dent in the wall came from the drag-out fight
that broke the bannister and left one whimpering boy
in a corner of his room for hours, terrified
by his own new rage.

How we've stomped and slithered this matted yarn.
"Roses bloom beneath our feet," my own mother used to hum
whenever we children quarreled. We came to hate that song,
its sickly sweetness. The embarrassment
of wishfulness. Wistfulness.

We won't pull out carpet again.
What, then, can I lay down
between fir strips and pad to anchor our remaining days
in this slippery letting go?
We chose this carpet for its strength,
and also its give.

What Her Missionary Son's Letter Didn't Say

Rain hangs in the air.
Even my underwear feels wet.

I listen to the tapping fingertips
of the bodies of bugs hitting netting
at night. Gray water. Bare floors.

My companion is
around.

The people
are more real
than anyone I've ever met—
than you, maybe,
in that long-ago world.

My companion won't sing.
This is the rainy season.

Flood

Try to catch the deluge in a paper cup.
—Crowded House

My childhood home's crack
in the foundation was felt and not seen, like God,
except once a year or so, when desert storm
would seep the carpet into sponge. The stench

of something not right. Rot
in the drywall, in the sodden pad
we pulled up corners of, placed
a fan behind, and tacked back down
a week later, pretending nothing
had happened, though every rain
resurrected the funk in the fiber,

memento mori. Flood
means too much to hold, means what can't
be channeled. New Orleans flood refugees, muddy,
flooded the shelters, clotting. One spring

my neighbors' basement flooded—that invisible crack.
A month later, they separated. Too much seepage,
not enough towels in the world. A bloodflow

from the wrong side of my heart
makes a clot, a stroke, the absence of a flood
of memories. A hot damn. One year,

church services in our town were cancelled, the righteous
excused to sandbag State Street, channeling

an impromptu canal away from sewers
designed for a desert. We changed the channel. On TV,

another desert; refugees clot the camps.
Change the channel.
A bruise is a flood
beneath flesh.
Not enough towels in the world.

Tower of Babel

We didn't really nowtice what was happening at first. It was so gradual. The dropping of a word's inding, the slurring, a slanted accent. We crocked our heads, asked each other to ropeat things. You don't believe me, but think of the wry a tree rots slowly form the inside, the way it pits out fewer and fywer leaves but still seems to preside over the yard. A body slawly curls in on idself over thirty years, bud so many good days and bad dais pile up you don't see the prend until you find yourself avolding stairs. A marriage is busy, then a business, and than islands skrifting into patches on the holizon. Things dicay.

Soneone finarry asked the question, pointed out that we were sorking at crocc-purposes. There were neetings. There were tantruns. Peopre denanded nore wages, began circurating peditions, then resumes. One tay we noticet that the bik bosses were apsent, having retiret ant novet out to Nartha's Vineyart. Nittle nanagepent nanaget varialtry to keep up abborances, cawwing in temps, but by Judae nost peopwe hat seed the writhing on the waw. After arr the union trateworkers hat novet on, the wast to heave was a ninor poritician with big dreans ant his pur secretary he hat proniset to norry as soon as his tivorce went thraw. No one locket the toor.

What wo woarnot was nothing I court oxprain to you, nothing you court ovor untorstant, unross first I court tako you to tho top ank thow you that fiow, hom lo tky skrotchot tro gworioutry uroink ut, hom chnuw our unniveng in-wuyt wookb. Ip hounkt ny dring gtiw.

We Go Camping During a Pandemic

Quiet like a flannel sheet, puddled at the edges.
The smell of woodsmoke and mountains
as antiseptic as bleach.
At night I face the smear of light behind the mountain,
imagine holding the city I left behind cupped in my palms.
I croon it a lullaby.

The arguing voices online
have disappeared into the whisper of lake lipping beach.
Under this moonlight, stark and astringent,
I remember that God loves each ardent voice, each
lurching politician.
How we fumble in this jumblesale world.

In the morning I rise early and walk briskly to atone
for being able to come here. I breathe deeply, stocking up
on dappled sun like toilet paper.
The aspens scintillate, "Pick me! Pick me!"
I pick them. I call on all of them. They call on me.

Teach me, please, how to return to community.
I must not leave unstaked
my corner of the greater tent.
But first, just a little more time in this one.

To My College Kids, Back at Home Because of Covid

You put on a brave face,
but I know you're grieving.

For *maybe*
you got *sort of*.

For a road with bends,
mirrored balls, the chance
glance, unlimited
bingo cards, each day
a new lottery ticket,
unscratched—

you got dryer lint,
an old Buick, "family
game night,"
jello.

No *what-if*s.
Instead, a long stretch of
anyways.

Not me.
Where I had thought I was sipping dregs,
plastic straw sputtering,
I got a free refill.
Like seeing tulips come up
in front of a house I bought in fall:
surprise!

Jackpot!
The run was extended

and I got discount tickets.

I should say I'm sorry—
my gain is your loss.
But I'm too busy scrambling to catch
all these shiny quarters.

Launch

50 years tiptoeing this whirligig
has left her achy from the pull. What's the prize
for the back-arching brace of it, chaotic brake of this
trundling trial to hold
everything together?
She's made up her mind. See her now

wind up for the fling—
no sissy-toss from a curly-headed fiddle-
de-dee flirt but an all-out hurl, full
follow-through, spit. She throws
caution to the wind
then launches herself, too, grabbing
the why-not of it, the dash
and the dip of it, leaping
before she looks.

Whirling and brewing, she's
fiercing and truing, over and throughing
and just watch her fly!
Thunder her under her shoulderblades, glide her
up the dancing dust-devil like a kite,
then cut the string.
She's figured out which way this second wind blows,
and she's out of here, streaming
across the sky like a shooting
star in its final flash,
its glorious burn.

Hot Flash

Minx in spanx, mincing as she goes,
or *memento mori* in sweatpants and ponytail,
it creeps up on me like someone walking
on my grave, the shadow of a plane
between me and the sun, a bad berry,
the bell that tolls for me, *carpé diem*, etc.
A skip in the record, hiccup in the groove.

Shut up. I'm not done dancing.
The best belly-dancers are older women, pant-
omiming birthing, earth
goddesses, crones. I will not heed
this gong, this honk of geese in dusk
this waa-waa-waa muted trumpet sit-com
laugh-track cue. I'm no red-nosed red-wigged
clown tripping over his shoes for a bow,
hooked cane approaching from stage left.
This is a call, bubba, a muster to head for the hills
and run with the wolves. Later, alligator.

IV

. . . its glorious burn . . .

Jane, While Beth

Jane, while Beth
sings to her children, always
arrives on time,

                        points out crickets and stars,
                                  floats on breezes.
                              Beth, while Jane
keeps her children calm in restaurants,
braids and purls,

                        preserves with tenderness,
                              weaves and curls.

                         Jane sits loose and easy,
                              maple syrup,
                           burlap and daisies,

while Beth stands straight and regal,
cellophane, dew and glitter.

Beth never learned to drive a stick.

                              Jane is tone-deaf.
Fresh-turned soil.

                               Non-stick pans.

Beth and Jane are milk and moon, darned and tucked,
guitar-licked, wild, plucked.

                    Jane and Beth are thick-thighed
              and airy, weedy and buttery, world-
                           wild and tangy.
            Breathless. Reckless.
            Woman.

At Age 50, She Buys Pink Roller-Skates

OK, OK, it was cliché—
the Mormon housewife budget version
of the mullet and Harley, the dramatic career change.
Which is to say, midlife crisis.
But it was something else, too.

For one thing, it was spring.
After an ugly winter, a winter of ugly
politics and ugly disease, and ugly
politics about the disease,
and diseased politics and chronic unease,

the eye yearned for light, for bright,
and so when she saw that black was out of stock
she knew that pink was fate, kismet,
exactly what the universe intended.

Bright pink, with lemon laces, looking
like candy, those Laffy Taffys in the bottom bin
at the 7-11 she'd passed every day on the way
home from school, 3-for-a quarter and 3
would last until she got home,
mouth sticky with sunshine,
those days before she'd lost "play"
because play had become her job.

These skates would feel like candy, she thought,
and clicked to add-to-cart the bright
pink wrist guards and knee pads, too,
knowing she would be a Spectacle in her suburban
cul-de-sac but daring herself like a teenager

at a stop light on Main, 10 p.m. on a summer night,
a car of cute boys in the next lane.

A week later, her teenagers held up
cameras, laughing, as she skated
around the kitchen island to disco tunes
like a breeze from a new direction in May.
They remembered
that she used to sing at the top of her lungs
sometimes. They remembered
that she was pretty.

Mother's Day in the Spirit World

The men stay indoors. The women, all sisters, walk out of front doors and tell no one where they're going or when they'll be back. They join arms like Red-Rover and sing, trilling fingers through everything. They eat chocolate, watch the kiss scene from *A Room With a View*. They take naps under weeping willows. They visit their living. They stroke the hair of tired mothers and whisper, "You make the sun rise—look how everyone's eyes follow you." To those who want to be mothers they whisper, "You are enough." To those who don't want to be mothers they whisper, "You are a blessing to the universe." To old women they say, "You're beautiful and God can't wait to see you again." To young girls they say, "Want the whole world and take it." They sprinkle laughter into dust devils and the ocean and all wind chimes and roller skates. They tickle babies. They tease out lilacs and waterfall spray. They tumble into thunder, bubble into plums.

Your Broken Heart Over Your Son's Broken Heart

Bite your tongue. You're no flyleaf
to his pain. Sure, you loved her, too, your heart
over-stretched like old pantyhose.
And so his ex will fade into the world, and so
you want to swaddle him again.

A mother's heart
is an overfull refrigerator, stale
and iffy, full of limp takeout cartons,
guilty and unrecyclable.
It is tacky cargo pants, utilitarian
and scratchy. Made of grass
and tchotchkes, dirt-bedraggled,
half-buried under the lilacs, a mother's heart

is one of the things you should never include in poems,
like God and sick puppies.

You dwell, as sentimental as a mime,
in the gap between Cinderella and Fairy Godmother.

As a child you put plastic dolls to bed,
lining up Barbie's shoes by color on your windowsill.
The fistfuls of dandelions you presented
your own mother have morphed
into a silent lurking in the doorway
of a sleeping manchild.

Either way,
it's you with your hand outstretched,
longing.

A Prayer

Dear God,

   Like this?

Prayer Language

We are to add *est* and *eth* to every verb, a tradition
leftover from a time when the words
meant *dearest, love of my life.* Now,
they are meant to make the language holy
(sacred, not secret), set apart
like a sabbath. *Thou art.* Apparently, I shouldn't love you
the same way I love gelato or the call
of a chickadee on a lonely afternoon,
as if they weren't the same thing.
At church, children and newcomers
talk to you straight out, not yet suspecting
how strange this sounds to us long-time worshippers,
how exciting. Once they realize, they blush and stutter,
adding letters indiscriminately.
I'm done with it.
It's like wearing boxing gloves for our thumb-matches, God,
and I won't have it. *Thou art* puts you in the sky somewhere,
and the sky is only half the story. You
are my hero and my nemesis and everything
in between. You are my heartbeat
and distant drums, my breath
and the glamorous squabble of aspen and spruce
on the mountainside. You abide
like the sequels of blockbusters, all of them
with you in the title: "Return of." "Revenge of."
You are subject and object, rain and blood.
Darling.

Temples in the Temple

Today my body-temple is bedraggled.
I've trundled it here like an ailing donkey,
dressed it and parked it, drifted and sloppy.

This is not a bad place for a nap.
Around me, some heads nod.
All of these temples, parked.
Some quiver, some overflow the seats.
Some sigh and tap and repeatedly clear their throats.

They are my body, too.
Together we are the temple,
ascending to Zion two hours at a time.

The old man and the old lady and the blousy overly-made-up
    lady and the
young lady with her hair ratted up and the gum-chewing lady
and the arthritis-gnarled hands.

Things I notice: the women's wedding rings
on the upraised hands in front of me
the downy youthfulness of the actors, so excited about LIFE.
The bodies—the dregs and branchings, the windblown aching
salty cragged texture all around me, sweat and drool
and tears and the blowing of a nose, the tapping of a foot,
all strapped into a starship out of here.

All of us face forward, facing something
for which we've brought tags, little flags,
little upraised hands begging for help.

I make promises I don't understand.
My body participates. I slouch and pooch, mind wafting
around the room, this immaculate, over-
air-conditioned room
made of drywall and prone to dust
like all of us.
Praise God.

Watching My Husband Play Softball

Twenty-five years, different towns,
different bleachers.
Mini-van years when I chased toddlers,
then years of our own cheering section.
Now again I sit alone,
bottom spreading farther on the bench.

Here in the pink dusk it's easy
to slip in time, both of us fresh
and bright again, you as the sun
in my eyes—but I wouldn't go back.
So many good years, and those darling
wrinkles around your eyes.

Watching you run, old man, still makes
my heart beat faster, not always in a good way.
You dive for a catch and, like a child
holding a kite-string, I thrill, of two
minds about the whipping wind.
Please return intact.

You have the same little-boy excitement
for each game, forgetting again
you'll be sore for days. When you run,
I see "mine" and "never mine," like the sky.

Walking back to the car, you clutching
your favorite bat and I the blanket,
we could be any two kids riding off
into the sunset, our old familiar room
and the landing-pad of our mattress
as good as any dazzling horizon to me,
and as warm.

Date Night is Takeout and Netflix

You've learned to show up at 5 to avoid the lines.
There are things you know at this age.

To agree on the same place after all these years
is a humble and tender comfort.
You could order for each other.

You could go to a nicer place, if you wanted to.
There are things you know at this age.
Anna, the girl who works Friday nights,
knows your orders—fried rice for him, chow mein for her—
and gives you extra fortune cookies.

In the car, you do not talk much. 27 years together;
you are pleasantly tired. At this age,
you are home.

You know you need dish soap and dental floss and avocados
but you do not stop at the store. It's Date Night.
At this age, there are things you know.
You do not need plastic wrap, batteries, toothpicks,
upholstery stain-remover, weedkiller, or dryer sheets,
all of which trail after you like tinsel
on a January Christmas tree on its way to the dump.

You have sons, big boys who may
or may not be making progress in this world.
The sons are busy on Friday nights,
so you bring food home and watch police dramas together
with the younger cat, who prefers his lap and her plate.
There is an older cat you wish would die soon.
There are things you admit at this age.

You have each other, in various ways
and to various extents.
If you do not like the fortune in your cookie, you take his,
assuming it was meant for you. This delights him.
It could be a metaphor.

You watch and watch until bleary,
then hold each other in the dark.
You are lonely, together and apart,
but only a little.
There are things you know at this age.

Heading to the Cabin, Heber, Utah

Once inside the canyon, note the change.
Shading into cool, the air is soft,
the wind descending from the glacier like
an angel with a message. Watch for deer
and other revelations. Pass the posh
and orchestrated mansions that infest
the ski slopes—we'll have none of that fool's gold
embangled fakery today. Move on.
Climb a couple summits, then it's all
downhill. The foothills melt into pastures;
the cows and sheep sail by in apathy
like clouds. Slow, now—here comes the turn.
The spitting gravel signals the home stretch.
Let the bouncing jolt you free, shake off
the barnacles of that other world of rush
and paperwork. The rhythm peels you clean
and lulls you into aspen. You've arrived.

The Refrigerator Clicks On

String them like beads, the times I've heard that sound,
the kitchens, the tables, the waiting:

      My mother's back to me,
my breath on a window,
taste of soggy thumb,
the familiar scratch in the surface
of the table, my cheek on my arm,
hair in my eyes.

      Then books and papers,
bricklike textbooks tethering me
when I want to be out there,
anywhere else, living what I think
must be life.

      Then suddenly a sleeping baby in a high chair
painted with peas and peaches,
my forehead on the tablecloth
of eternal afternoon.

      Sometimes, the space between us,
between what I can't believe
I said and you said
and what you said I said
and didn't.

All the moments
the garage door doesn't go up
while a teenager is still out.
Crossword puzzles, solitaire,
deep breaths.

Thanksgiving dinner,
all the faces,
and afterwards, the space
after the last door closes
for the washing of dishes
with all the time in the world.

God as a Verb

God, to me, it seems, is a verb not a noun, proper or improper.
—Buckminster Fuller

What does it mean, this "Godding"? Is "to God"
a transitive verb, and if so, am I subject or object?

I try out as subject, wielding God as magic wand.
I god my world-weary teenager's whines

with mixed results. I God the fact
that he needs new sneakers

and that he has lost his winter coat again.
I God the clogged toilet, the frozen

stray cat who died beneath the porch. I try
to God the party where I'm shy and miserable

but fail and go home early. Let me
wrench myself, then, into object. God me,

sweet blue morning that follows awkward nights.
God me, U2 in the elevator, grin of my boy

as he tells me a joke. Yea, even you, doctor's bill,
oil leak—even politics on Facebook. I will conjugate

my Godding, subjunct myself holy.
By breathing be breathed, by turning

be turned. Consider the dandelions of the field,
how they, by Godding the breeze,

become in turn Godded, haze
of downy glory, numberless as stars.

The Mirrored Ball Never Gets Taken Down

Each morning God saunters over to me, shy wallflower,
and boldly extends his hand.
We dance. Sometimes I put on my flared skirt
and polka at the picnic, reel at the barbecue.
But some days I drift about in stained sweat pants
slumping against him like a fifteen-year-old
with mean parents and a curfew.

Still, every morning, he shows up, jerks
his head meaningfully towards the dance floor
and I keep reaching out my hand.
Each night he returns me singed and yawning,
but sometimes summons me three hours later
for the meteor shower fussy baby pajama hoky-poky.

I will hell yes. I will hail dance, drum circle.
Even as my heavy feet and heavy heart stumble
no-no-no with each systole, I will diastole back yes, yes, yes,
tush-push and boot-scoot. Yes
to the twirls. Yes, even, to the heart-
dropping dips, the chicken walk,
holy macarena.

Notes

Epigraph, p. xi
From "Here," by Grace Paley, in *Good Poems*, ed. Garrison Keillor.
   New York: Penguin, 2002.

"The Young Men Go River-Rafting for a Week"
Epigraph from "Orientation," in *Good Bones* by Maggie Smith.
   North Adams, MA: Tupelo Press, 2017.

"Flood"
Epigraph from "Don't Dream It's Over" by Crowded House, in
   Crowded House, Capitol Records, 1986. Album.

Translation:

We didn't really notice what was happening at first. It was so gradual. The dropping of a word's ending, the slurring, a slanted accent. We cocked our heads, asked each other to repeat things. You don't believe me, but think of the way a tree rots slowly from the inside, the way it puts out fewer and fewer leaves but still seems to preside over the yard. A body slowly curls in on itself over thirty years, but so many good days and bad days pile up you don't see the trend until you find yourself avoiding stairs. A marriage is busy, and then a business, and then islands drifting into patches on the horizon. Things decay.

Someone finally asked the question, pointed out that we were working at cross-purposes. There were meetings. There were tantrums. People demanded more wages, began circulating petitions, then resumes. One day we noticed that the big bosses were absent, having retired and moved out to Martha's Vineyard. Middle management managed valiantly to keep up appearances, calling in temps, but by July most people had seen the writing on the wall. After all the union tradeworkers had moved on, the last to leave was a minor politician with big dreams and his poor secretary he had promised to marry as soon as his divorce went through. No one locked the door.

What we learned was nothing I could explain to you, nothing you could ever understand, unless first I could take you to the top and show you that view, how the sky stretched so gloriously around us, how small our annoying in-laws looked. It haunts my dreams still.

"God as a Verb"
Epigraph by R. Buckminster Fuller, in *Secondhand God and Other Writings.* Carbondale, IL: Southern Illinois University Press, 1963.

Acknowledgements

These poems have appeared, some in a slightly different form, in the following publications. I'm grateful to their editors for giving these poems a first home.

"First Argument" *BYU Studies*
"A Plan of Salvation" *Irreantum*
"My Friend's Marriage is Failing But I'm Not Supposed to Know" *Young Ravens Literary Review*
"A Good Sick Girl Never Gives Up" *Dialogue*
"Christmas" *The Spirit of the Season*, Aspen Books, ed. Curtis Taylor
"Shoveling II: 5 a.m. Salt Lake City Suburb" *LDS Living*
"Replacing the Carpet in the Emptying Nest" *Common Ground*
"Tower of Babel" *Mormon Lit Blitz*
"At Age 50, She Buys Pink Roller-Skates" *Young Ravens Literary Review*
"Prayer Language" *Wayfare*
"I Wanna Be God's Back-up Singer" *Literature and Belief*

DARLENE YOUNG's first poetry collection, *Homespun and Angel Feathers* (BCC Press, 2019), won the Association for Mormon Letters award for poetry. A recipient of the Smith-Pettit Foundation Award for Outstanding Contribution to Mormon Letters and BYU's Adjunct Faculty Publication Award, she teaches creative writing at Brigham Young University. She has served as poetry editor of *Dialogue* and *Segullah*. Her work has been noted in *Best American Essays* and nominated for Pushcart Prizes. She lives in South Jordan, Utah.

Made in United States
Troutdale, OR
12/14/2023

15852898R00066